THE LITTLE BOOK OF

ALLOTMENT

TIPS

William Fortt

THE LITTLE BOOK OF

ALLOTMENT

TIPS

William Fortt

A.

'I want death to find me planting my cabbages'

Michel de Montaigne (1533–1592),
French philosopher and essayist

1. **A good allotment is worth waiting for, so be patient.** Hold out for the allotment which is best and most convenient for you, rather than being in a rush to grab the first plot which becomes available.

" A good allotment is worth
waiting for, so be patient. "

2.

How do you find an allotment?
First of all, contact your local council and ask them. If they have nothing available, try the National Society of Allotment and Leisure Gardeners (www.nsalg.org.uk) or the Federation of City Farms and Community Gardens (www.farmgarden.org.uk).

"How do you find an allotment?"

3. Ask around the neighbourhood. If all else fails, try inquiring locally. **Many people have spare plots of land they might be prepared to rent out to an enthusiastic gardener** (even a beginner). So talk to neighbours, workmates, local farmers and friends. You never know what might come up.

"Many people have spare plots of land they might be prepared to rent out to an enthusiastic gardener."

4. **Find an allotment as near your home as possible.** The shorter the journey the better – especially important if you have to tend plants every day (think of watering in dry summers). You'll enjoy your gardening all the more if getting there is not too bothersome.

"Find an allotment as near your home as possible."

5. **Get a transport system worked out.** A car or at least a bicycle may be essential. **Remember, everything for the plot will have to be carried there.** This includes tools, seeds and watering cans as well as bulky items like compost and hoses. **Then,** of course, **you'll have to carry the produce back home.**

"Get a transport system worked out. Remember, everything for the plot will have to be carried there. Then, you'll have to carry the produce back home."

6. Remember: gardening can take up a lot of your spare time. So, if your leisure is limited, **think about sharing a plot with someone else.** Either cultivate half the ground each, or divide the work equally on the whole thing. Choose someone you can trust to do their fair share of labour.

"Think about sharing a plot with someone else."

7.

Take a good hard look at the allotment site before you sign up.

Is there a convenient water supply? Is your plot likely to be a frost pocket in winter? In which direction is it facing? Will it be shaded by trees or hedges in summer? Is the ground liable to get waterlogged or flooded?

"Take a good hard look at the allotment site before you sign up."

8.

The most important question is: what's the soil like? Get a rough idea by picking up a fistful and squashing it into a ball. If it sticks firmly together, it's clay. If it falls apart, it's sandy. These need improving with composts and other materials. If you're lucky, you'll have a nice dark loamy soil – not too sticky, not too dry.

"The most important question is: what's the soil like?"

9. **Get to know your fellow allotment holders.** They'll usually be happy to answer many of the queries mentioned in Tips #7 and #8 – and a lot more. The older hands will know about local problems (such as the likelihood of vandalism). Most gardeners are glad to dispense wisdom, advice and the odd seedling.

"**Get to know your fellow allotment holders.**"

10.

You may inherit an overgrown plot, full of brambles and other perennial horrors. If it's a large area, **clear the soil little by little,** a manageable patch at a time – but do the job thoroughly. Once a patch is weed-free and bare, you can start sowing or planting it.

"You may inherit an overgrown plot, clear the soil little by little.

11.

Good tools will last a lifetime, so buy the best you can afford. **The absolute essentials are: a fork and a spade; a rake, a hoe and a line with stakes at each end** to mark out rows. A watering can and a good pair of gardening gloves will help, too. And if you're growing fruit you'll need secateurs.

"The absolute essentials are: a fork and a spade; a rake, a hoe and a line with stakes at each end."

12. If your plot has a shed, **is it safe to leave tools and other equipment there?** As before, get advice from other gardeners. If in doubt, take the tools home every time. Another option is to make the fork and spade handles removeable. Thieves are unlikely to pinch handle-less tools.

"Is it safe to leave tools and other equipment there?"

13.

Make yourself comfortable.
At the very least, this means some kind of seat to rest on – a plank on upturned buckets will do. Better still, put up a cheap and simple shelter or shed to keep off showers or cold winds while you drink your tea.

Make yourself comfortable.

14.

For rough digging of untended ground, use a spade rather than a fork. Turn over a clod, then chop it to bits with the spade edge. Also use the spade to slice off the turfy top section and bury this upside down at the bottom of the trench, where it will be covered with the next lot of soil and slowly rot down.

"For rough digging of untended ground, use a spade."

15.

The obvious way to **get rid of weeds** is **by digging or pulling them out.** This is tough work, for you must be sure to extract all the roots of perennial weeds like couchgrass or bindweed, otherwise they'll appear again. But it's also effective and costs nothing – apart from sore knees or an aching back.

"Get rid of weeds by digging or pulling them out.

16. **The best weed suppressor is** a layer of **mulch. This smothers and kills almost everything.** It can be organic (compost, animal manure, or cardboard covered with a layer of soil), which breaks down into the soil, or inorganic (black plastic sheet or even old carpet), which doesn't.

"The best weed suppressor is mulch. This smothers and kills almost everything."

17.

Divide the plot into a series of deep beds. These are deeply dug (obviously), and **no more than 1.2m (4ft) wide.** This means you can reach the centre from either side and never have to tread on the dug soil. As a result, the soil never gets compacted, and remains easy to weed and fork through.

"Divide the plot into a series of deep beds no more than 1.2m wide.”

18.

Lay narrow paths between the beds.
This is what you'll walk or push
barrows on (instead of squashing
the dug soil). Hard paths are easier
to maintain than grass. Use broken
brick and stone, gravel or wood chips,
and edge with whole bricks or slates
to stop it spilling onto the soil.

"**Lay narrow paths between the beds.**"

19. **Perennial weeds can be treated with a chemical herbicide.** Remember that this should only be done in the growing season, when there are leaves to aim at. Otherwise the spray may be ineffective. In general, use chemicals of this sort as sparingly as possible.

"Perennial weeds can be treated with a chemical herbicide."

20.

Be prepared to diversify. If this is your only piece of garden, **you may want to produce more than just vegetables.** You could set aside an area for growing flowers, and another for soft fruit such as raspberries and blackcurrants. If you're planning a long stay, think about planting shrubs or even small fruit trees.

"Be prepared to diversify. You may want to produce more than just vegetables."

21. **Harvest the rain.** Drought is becoming more common, and you may be far from a tap. So **catch and store rainwater.** Buy a plastic water butt, or use anything handy, such as old oil drums or dustbins. If you have a shed, fix guttering and down pipes to direct the water to the tank.

"Harvest the rain. Catch and store rainwater.

22.

Know your vegetable families.
They can be roughly split into four main groups – potatoes, roots (carrots, turnips etc), brassicas (cabbages, sprouts etc) and the rest (which includes onions, lettuce, beans and peas). Each group has different growing needs, frailties and strengths.

"Know your vegetable families."

23. Know the rules and be considerate. Most allotment societies have a code of conduct. This may cover anything from restrictions on what you can grow to weed control and rubbish disposal. **Stick to the rules, and remember that thoughtless actions can ruin your neighbours' crops – and their tempers.**

"Stick to the rules, and remember that thoughtless actions can ruin your neighbours' crops – and their tempers.

24.

Rotation, rotation, rotation. If you grow one family of vegetables in the same place every year, specific diseases and pests will build up in the soil. So divide the plot into 4 sections and rotate what you grow in each – spuds one year, roots the next, onions and salads the next, and so on.

"Rotation, rotation, rotation."

25.

A compost heap is the heart of the garden. Knock up a bin from pallets or scrap wood, then fill it with garden waste. This includes kitchen leftovers (no citrus or meat), grass mowings, non-perennial weeds, torn card and newspaper, plus a sprinkling of earth. Turn the whole thing once and leave for 3 months.

"A compost heap is the heart of the garden.

26.

Keep improving your soil. Add as much humus (organic material) as you can, to help soil structure, and the ability to retain nutrients. Anything organic – composts, mulches, seaweed, grass mowings – will do a lot of good. Just spread them on top – earthworms will dig them in for you.

"Keep improving your soil."

27. Growing plants need food, in the form of nutrients. Compost only provides a fraction of this. **Make sure your soil has the correct balance of chemicals and trace elements.** It can get these from materials such as blood, fish and bone meal, animal manure, volcanic rock dust or a commercial fertilizer.

"Make sure your soil has the correct balance of chemicals and trace elements."

28. **When a bed is dug, rake it thoroughly to get a fine and level tilth.** Get rid of stones, weed roots and other clutter. A well-raked surface makes it much easier to sow seeds evenly, and to pull out competing weeds later on. Good tilth also allows water to penetrate more evenly to the soil below.

"When a bed is dug, rake it thoroughly to get a fine and level tilth."

29.

Take the trouble to sow seeds at the correct distance and depth.
Spacing (between both individual plants and rows) has a big effect on plant growth. Plant potatoes too closely, for example, and the crop will be smaller. Follow the instructions on the seed packet, or consult a trustworthy gardening book.

"Take the trouble to sow seeds at the correct distance and depth."

30.

Make your own measuring stick for marking out rows. Find a thin piece of timber 2 metres (6½ ft) long. Using a tape measure, mark out metric measurements on one side (every 10 centimetres), with paint or a felt-tip pen. Then do the same for imperial measurements (in 3-inch units) on the other side.

Make your own measuring stick for marking out rows.

31.

You've measured your rows and scraped out furrows. **Before you sow the seeds, gently water the furrows.** This gets moisture into the soil under the seeds, ready to create a nice humid atmosphere to start them germinating. Use a can with a fine rose so that you don't flood the furrow and compact it.

"Before you sow the seeds,
gently water the furrows."

32.

Sow seeds as thinly as possible.
You don't want a tangled mat of shoots coming up, which needs major thinning out. This wastes seed and means you'll probably damage the remaining seedlings. Leave space between each seed. This is a fiddly job, but will give you stronger and healthier plants.

"Sow seeds as thinly as possible."

33. **Rake the soil gently back over the seeds in the furrows.** Be careful not to disturb the seeds by being too forceful. Tamp down the soil – just as gently – with the head of the rake. Then give the bed another light watering.

Rake the soil gently back over the seeds in the furrows.

34. **Remember to mark the rows.** Sounds obvious, but it's easy to forget exactly what you've sown as the weeks go by. Write the crop's name on a stick, or slot the empty seed packet into a split piece of bamboo. To be doubly sure, keep a written record as well, with the date of sowing.

Remember to mark the rows.

35.

Start brassicas and other winter vegetables in a seed bed in a spare corner of the allotment. Here you can raise seedlings without taking up space in the main beds. By summer, early potato and bean crops will be gone, so you can transplant seedlings from the seed bed to take their place.

Start brassicas and other winter vegetables in a seed bed.

36.

Be generous with water. Rather than just wetting the surface every day, give it a good long soak every 3 or 4 days. This means the moisture will soak right down to reach the roots of the plants, where it is really needed.

Be generous with water.

37. **Raspberries are an ideal fruit to grow in an allotment.** Not only do they crop heavily, they also make use of vertical space. Support them by tying to a series of wires stretched between two head-high posts. Summer-fruiting varieties have much the best flavour.

"Raspberries are an ideal fruit
to grow in an allotment."

38. **Currant bushes** take up a lot of space, but once established they will **give you wonderful crops year after year.** And they are a wonderful source of vitamin C. Plant black-, red- or whitecurrants 1.5m (5ft) apart and learn how to prune them properly (it's too complex to explain here).

Currant bushes give you wonderful crops year after year.

39.

Everybody loves strawberries. Unfortunately, so do snails, slugs and many other pests. **When the fruit appears, cushion the straggling stems on plenty of clean straw.** This keeps the fruit dry, and discourages mould, mildew and molluscs.

Everybody loves strawberries. When the fruit appears, cushion the straggling stems on plenty of clean straw.

40.

Planning to be a long-term allotment holder? Plant one or two fruit trees. **Apples, plums or pears on a dwarfing root stock will grow no higher than 4m (13ft), and bear fruit within 3 years.** Alternatively, train them against a wall or wire supports.

Apples, plums or pears on a dwarfing root stock will grow no higher than 4m (13ft), and bear fruit within 3 years.

41.

A cage will stop birds ruining your fruit crop. If bushes, canes and low trees are grouped together, you can cover them with a single fruit cage. Sink posts at the corners, link with thick wire, and cover the whole with plastic netting. Remember to include an access point so that you can gather the ripe fruit.

"A cage will stop birds ruining your fruit crop.

42. Always have something growing. **Use your allotment to its maximum capacity by following one crop with another** from March through until late autumn. Even in October you can sow carrots and beans, and plant winter salad leaves. Garlic can go in as late as December.

"Use your allotment to its maximum capacity by following one crop with another."

43.

Make your allotment child-friendly.
Kids usually love the glamorous jobs
like picking strawberries or peas.
Add to the fun with a paddling pool
or a swing. Set them jolly tasks like
making a scarecrow or painting plant
labels. Give them their own section of
garden, to grow whatever they like.

"**Make your allotment child-friendly.**"

44.

What's better than an allotment? Answer: two allotments! As knowledge and passion grow, you may find one plot is no longer big enough for you. If there are spare plots available, why not take on another? Now you'll have room for more fruit, more flowers – maybe even a chicken run.

What's better than an allotment? Answer: two allotments!

45.

Get discounts on your seeds. One massive advantage of belonging to an allotment association is that you can club together and make large seed orders. Many merchants offer as much as 50% discount on orders over a set value.

"Get discounts on your seeds."

46.

Mice love allotments – and so, unfortunately, do rats. Rodents cause damage and can spread disease, and must be controlled. The only effective solution is poison. Put the bait in secured lengths of drainpipe. Rats can't resist a tunnel, but most other animals will keep out.

"Mice love allotments – and so, unfortunately, do rats."

47. **How do you control slugs?** Pellets (the enviro-friendly kind) are effective killers, and so are shallow containers of beer. You can also keep the beasts out with a barrier of dry material such as sand or grit. It helps to keep the ground clear of weeds or long grass where they can shelter.

"How do you control slugs?"

48.

An allotment looks like a free banquet to birds – especially big scavengers like pigeons, rooks and gulls. So protect the most tempting crops (tomatoes, raspberries, peas, young brassicas etc) with narrow-mesh netting over hoops of willow or thick wire.

"An allotment looks like a free banquet to birds.

49.

Keep a weekly record of everything you do and grow. Compare your allotment and its produce year by year. This helps you to **spot your mistakes** and learn from them, and to **enjoy your successes.** A journal is also the best place to work out your plans for the future.

"Keep a weekly record... Spot your mistakes... Enjoy your successes.

50.

An allotment is about more than growing food. It's a place to get closer to the earth and nature. Bring wildlife to your plot – flowers and scented shrubs like buddleia attract insects, and berry or seed-bearing plants draw the birds. A pond is a magnet for frogs and many other wee creatures.

"An allotment is about more than growing food."

William Fortt

William Fortt is **a gardener of long standing,** whose
cottage garden in Wiltshire is famed for the beauty of
its rare plants and the wonders of its many varieties of
culinary and medicinal herbs. He has been an author
for more than 30 years, with many books to his name.

"**A gardener of long standing.**"

**Little Books of Tips from
Absolute Press**

Aga
Allotment
Avocado
Beer
Cake Decorating
Cheese
Coffee
Fishing

Gardening
Gin
Golf
Herbs
Spice
Tea
Whisky
Wine

If you enjoyed this book, try...

THE LITTLE BOOK OF

GARDENING

TIPS

"If you're going away on holiday, take measures to keep your house plants moist and happy."

"It's very easy to repair damaged edges of your lawn."

ABSOLUTE PRESS

An imprint of Bloomsbury Publishing Plc

50 Bedford Square   1385 Broadway
London   New York
WC1B 3DP   NY 10018
UK   USA

www.bloomsbury.com

ABSOLUTE PRESS and the A. logo are trademarks of Bloomsbury Publishing Plc

First published in 2012
This edition printed 2018

Cover image: Dorling Kindersley, Will Heap / Getty Images

A catalogue record for this book is available from the British Library.
Library of Congress Cataloguing-in-Publication data has been applied for.
ISBN 13: 9781472954459

Printed and bound in Spain by Tallers Grafics Soler